The Magic Pencil

Written by Chris Lutrario
Illustrated by Jan Nesbitt

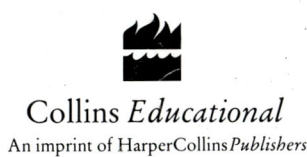

Collins *Educational*
An imprint of HarperCollins*Publishers*

Once upon a time, in a land far away, there lived a girl called Gretchen. Now Gretchen loved to draw, but she was too poor to buy a pencil.

So Gretchen drew pictures in the sand with a stick. She drew pictures in the mud with her finger. She scratched pictures on rocks with a little stone.

One day, Gretchen said to herself, "I wish I had a pencil. Then I could draw beautiful pictures and give them to the people in the village."

Suddenly, an old man with a long white beard appeared. He spoke to Gretchen in a gentle voice.

"Do not be afraid. Here is a pencil for you. But remember. Use it only to draw pictures for the people of your village."

Then, just as suddenly, the old man disappeared.

Gretchen picked up the pencil and drew a picture of a cat.

No sooner had she finished drawing, than the cat leapt off the paper, twined itself around her legs and began to purr.

"Extraordinary!" said Gretchen,
"This must be a magic pencil."
She walked through the village.
She saw a woman picking apples.
But the woman could not reach the
apples on the topmost branches of
the tree.

"I know what you need," said Gretchen. And she drew a picture of a ladder. No sooner had she finished drawing, than her picture turned into a real ladder.

The woman climbed up and picked the apples on the topmost branches.

Gretchen went on her way.
Soon she met a man digging a field.
It was hard, slow work.

"I know what you need," said Gretchen. And she drew a picture of an ox and a plough.

No sooner had she finished drawing, than her picture turned into a real ox and a real plough.
The man harnessed the ox to the plough, and set out across the field.

Every day, Gretchen walked around the village, drawing pictures of things that the people needed.

Now, it was not long before news of Gretchen's magic pencil spread far and wide throughout the land. Soon the King heard about it and sent his soldiers to find Gretchen.

They took her to the King's palace.

The King said to Gretchen, "Draw me a tree with gold coins growing on it."
"No," said Gretchen. "I will not.
I use my pencil only to draw things that the people in my village need. They are poor. You are not. You do not need any gold coins."

The king was furious.
"Do you dare to disobey me, you wicked girl? I shall lock you up in the deepest, darkest dungeon."
So the King's soldiers took Gretchen away and locked her in the deepest, darkest dungeon.
"I know what I need," said Gretchen.

And she drew a picture of a key. No sooner had she finished drawing, than her picture turned into a real key. She opened the door and escaped.

The King and his soldiers jumped on their horses and rode after Gretchen. Soon they were close behind her.

"I know what I need," said Gretchen. And she drew a picture of an enormous hole.

No sooner had she finished drawing, than her picture turned
into a real hole.

The King and his soldiers were galloping too fast to stop. They rode straight into the hole, and were never seen again.

As for Gretchen, she ran all the way home. And from that day on she lived happily in her village, drawing anything and everything the people needed.